In Japan

written by **Judy Zocchi** illustrated by **Neale Brodie**

dingles & company New Jersey

For Michael Ning

©2005 by Judith Mazzeo Zocchi

First printing

PUBLISHED BY dingles&company
P.O. Box 508 • Sea Girt, New Jersey • 08750
WEBSITE: www.dingles.com • E-MAIL: info@dingles.com

Library of Congress Catalog Card No.: 2004094736
ISBN: 1-59646-004-0

Printed in the United States of America

ART DIRECTION & DESIGN BY Barbie Lambert
ENGLISH EDITED BY Andrea Curley
RESEARCH AND ADDITIONAL COPY WRITTEN BY Robert Neal Kanner
EDUCATIONAL CONSULTANT Bridget Riley Turnbach
ART ASSISTANTS Erin Collity & Sara Sagliano
PRE-PRESS BY Pixel Graphics

The Global Adventures series takes children on an around-the-world exploration of a variety of fascinating countries. The series examines each country's history and physical features as well as its most popular customs, activities, and foods.

Global Adventures

Judy Zocchi

is the author of the Global Adventures, Holiday Happenings, Click & Squeak's Computer Basics, and Paulie and Sasha series. She is a writer and lyricist who holds a bachelor's degree in fine arts/theater from Mount Saint Mary's College and a master's degree in educational theater from New York University. She lives in Manasquan, New Jersey, with her husband, David.

Neale Brodie

is a freelance illustrator who lives in Brighton, England, with his wife and young daughter. He is a self-taught artist, having received no formal education in illustration. As well as illustrating a number of children's books, he has worked as an animator in the computer games industry.

In Japan money is called the YEN.

Japanese currency is called the yen. This means "circle" in Japanese.

JAPANESE
is the spoken word.

*Japanese is the main language of Japan.
It is spoken by 99 percent of the people.*

Who has been to Kyoto?
I have!

SUMO WRESTLING
is a favorite sport.

Sumo wrestling is an ancient Japanese sport. It takes place in a round area called a dohyo. The first wrestler to touch the ground either inside or outside of the circle loses.

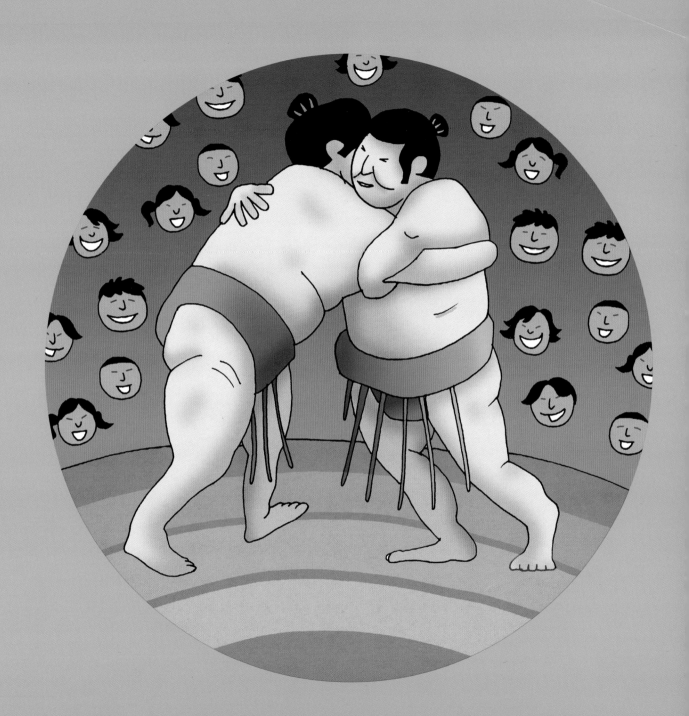

The CRANE
is the national bird.

Cranes are big, long-necked, long-legged birds that live in marshes and wetlands. In Japan they are considered a symbol of long life.

In Japan most people eat with CHOPSTICKS.

Chopsticks are the traditional eating utensils of Japan. They are a pair of pointed sticks that are usually made of wood, bamboo, or metal.

A MANGA
is a comic book.

Manga is the Japanese version of an American comic book. Manga are published on a wide variety of topics for people of all ages. There are manga cookbooks, biographies, novels, and textbooks.

KENDO

is a martial art.

Kendo is the traditional martial art of Japanese fencing. Players fence with bamboo practice swords (shinai) and try to hit targets on their opponent's armor. Kendo means "way of the sword" in Japanese.

People serve RICE with most meals they cook.

Rice is a very important crop for Japan and has been cultivated there for more than 2,000 years. Japanese rice is short grained and becomes sticky when cooked.

In Japan some people sleep on FUTONS.

A *futon* is a flat Japanese mattress. When unrolled on a *tatami* (straw floor mat), it becomes a bed. It is usually rolled up and put away during the day.

And some BOW to say hello.

Japanese say hello to each other by bowing. Bowing is also used for thanking someone or apologizing.

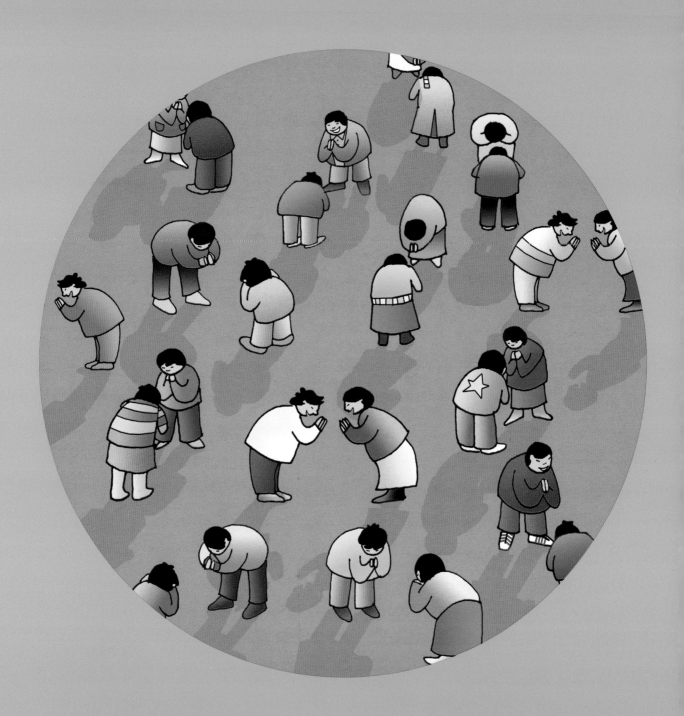

A KIMONO is a loosely tied robe.

A kimono is one type of traditional Japanese clothing made of silk. Nowadays, kimonos are mainly worn at special or formal occasions such as weddings, tea ceremonies, and funerals.

BUNRAKU
is a puppet show.

Bunraku is a traditional form of Japanese theater. The puppets are about 3½ feet tall, and up to three puppeteers work each of them. One person does all the puppets' voices.

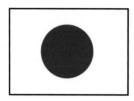

Japanese culture is fun to learn.

YEN

JAPANESE

SUMO WRESTLING
(su-moh)

CRANE

CHOPSTICKS

MANGA
(man-gah)

KENDO
(KEN-doh)

RICE

FUTONS
(fu-TONS)

BOW

KIMONO
(kee-MO-noh)

BUNRAKU
(BUN-rah-ku)

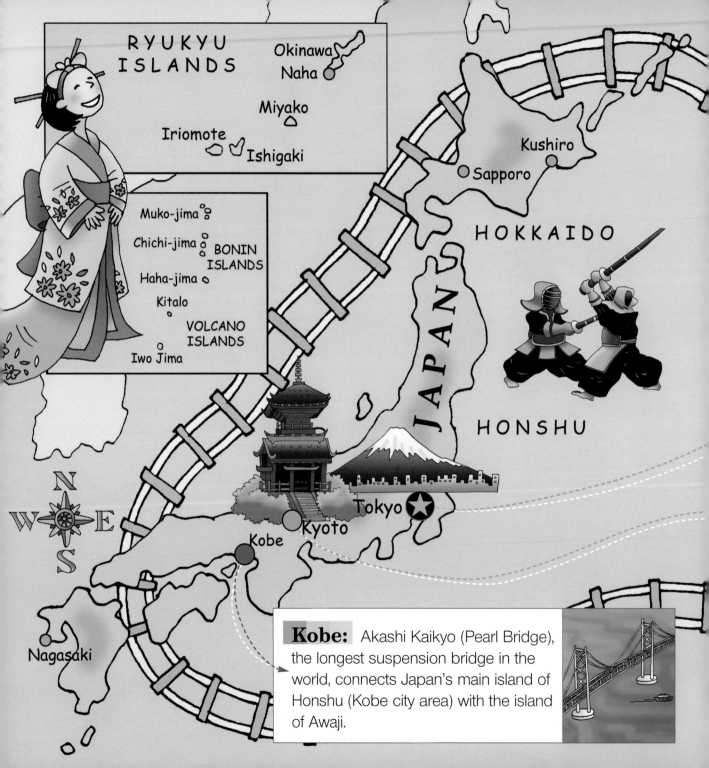

RYUKYU ISLANDS

Okinawa
Naha

Miyako

Iriomote
Ishigaki

Muko-jima
Chichi-jima
BONIN ISLANDS
Haha-jima
Kitalo
VOLCANO ISLANDS
Iwo Jima

Kushiro
Sapporo

HOKKAIDO

JAPAN

HONSHU

Tokyo

Kyoto

Kobe

N
W   E
S

Nagasaki

Kobe: Akashi Kaikyo (Pearl Bridge), the longest suspension bridge in the world, connects Japan's main island of Honshu (Kobe city area) with the island of Awaji.

Tokyo: You can see Japan's highest mountain, Mt. Fuji, if you look to the west of the city. In Japan, it's a sign of good luck just to get a glimpse of this mountain.

Kyoto: This is the cultural center of Japan, known for its many temples and shrines.

See what you can discover at every turn!

ABOUT JAPAN

Emperors were the traditional rulers of Japan from 710 until 1867. While they devoted their time to study, a new power arose–the samurai, or warrior class. These warrior families were headed by the shogun (military governors). They ruled Japan for many years. In the late sixteenth century, Christian missionaries and traders arrived from the West. The shogun rulers thought they came to conquer Japan and limited all contact with the outside world for 200 years. Over time the government became corrupt and the emperor resumed control. In 1854, Commodore Matthew Perry of the U.S. Navy helped reopen Japan to the West. Japan eventually became a military power. Japan invaded China in 1937, and the U.S. and England stopped trading certain goods with the Japanese. Japan saw this as an act of war and on December 7, 1941, attacked the American fleet at Pearl Harbor. Japan then invaded other countries in Southeast Asia and the Pacific. America and its allies sent troops to fight the Japanese. This war went on for four years until the U.S. ended it by dropping atomic bombs on Hiroshima and Nagasaki. Today Japan has a democratic government. Many popular cultural traditions come from Japan, including martial arts and origami (paper folding).

OFFICIAL NAME:
Japan

CAPITAL CITY:
Tokyo

CURRENCY:
Yen

MAJOR LANGUAGE:
Japanese

BORDERS:
Pacific Ocean, Sea of Japan

CONTINENT: Asia

UNDERSTANDING AND CELEBRATING CULTURAL DIFFERENCES

- What do you have in common with children from Japan?
- What things do you do differently from the children in Japan?
- What is your favorite new thing you learned about Japan?
- What unique thing about your culture would you like to share?

TRAVELING THROUGH JAPAN

- Which way would you be traveling if you went from Hiroshima to Kyoto?
- Name three countries that are to the north of Japan.
- On which of Japan's islands would you find Mt. Fuji?

TRY SOMETHING NEW...

Spend a day saying hello in Japanese! Greet your friends and neighbors by saying "Konichiwa" (koh-NEE-cheewah). Don't forget to bow!

For more information on the Global Adventures series or to find activities that coordinate with it, explore our website at **www.dingles.com**.